Teach a Tiny Tot to Read

LETTER AND PHONICS GAMES FOR EARLY READING

written by

Bonnie Macmillan

readin1week

First published in France in 2023 by readin1week

Trade paperback ISBN 978-1-9999663-5-5

The *Tiny Tot* books are dedicated to my late father
who loved children and enjoyed playing
all manner of games with them.

Tiny Tot books have seven READ RIGHT AWAY elements

1. An Early Start in Reading

Especially targeted at children aged 3 to 7 because the earlier a child succeeds in learning to read, the greater are the long-term benefits.

2. Step-by-Step Instructions

Simple, easy-to-follow instructions. No training and no teaching experience required!

3. Learning via Fun and Games

Fun, games and humour trigger the release of positive endorphins, hormones that act on the brain to maximize learning.

4. Motivating

A parent's praise and a flow of rewards make a child positively glow! Your child will be excited and keen to learn more!

5. Stress-free

Children and parents can proceed at their own pace.

6. Confidence—Boosting Sequence

Games are carefully sequenced to ensure your child's consistent success.

7. Foolproof

Innovative instruction is based on the latest scientific evidence. Every moment of a parent's time is used to the best effect.

Teach a Tiny Tot to Read

Letter and Phonics Games for Early Reading

STEP 4: MEENA MOOSE

Contents

THE TINY TOT BOOKS

STEP 1 **Annabel Ant**	STEP 4 **Meena Moose**	STEP 7 **Giddy Goat**
STEP 2 **Benjamin Bat**	STEP 5 **Champ the Chimp**	STEP 8 **Tiger Shark**
STEP 3 **Calico Cat**	STEP 6 **Dale a Whale**	STEP 9 **Oakley Owl**

Introduction

Welcome to the Step 4 book of the *Tiny Tot* series, an important milestone.

- After playing the games in this book, your child will know how to read ***more than half*** of all the 42 sounds heard in English.

The *Tiny Tot* books teach the letter-to-sound relationships starting with the most useful and common ones. So far, your child knows 18 of them. This book will introduce your child to another six

With the letters learned so far, there is a nearly perfect one-to-one correspondence between a letter and its sound. But there are only 26 letters in the alphabet. There are not enough letters to represent all the 42 sounds heard in English! To solve this, sometimes *two* letters are used to represent a new sound. This book introduces that concept for the first time.

Let's Get Started!

FIVE kinds of games in this book train the necessary reading skills:

1. Letter Shape Sharpeners

The aim of these games is to fine-tune your child's visual skills so that he will be able recognize the different letter shapes fast.

2. Letter-Talking Tales

The purpose of these games is to teach your child the sounds that letter shapes 'say'. Children understand the concept that people talk so they can understand the concept that letters 'talk' too.

3. Lightning Letter-Sounds

These games train your child to translate letters into their sounds with increasing ease and speed.

4. Mind-Bending Blending

These games teach your child how to 'sound out' the letters in words one by one and how to blend the sounds together.

5. Wickedly Wily Word Reading

The aim of these entertaining games is to entice your child to practise reading words, phrases and stories.

Books to Read: 1) *Peek-A-Boo* 2) *1, 2, 3 Swim in the Pool*

WELCOME TO THE STEP 4 TINY TOT GAMES!

Simple: Simply play the games in the order they appear.

Short: Keep your play sessions short — 15 to 20 minutes.

Praise: Give your child plenty of praise and heartfelt hugs.

Compliment: Tell your child how clever you think he/she is.

Practise: Feel free to repeat any games for more practice.

Rewards: Have a good supply on hand (hugs, stickers, snacks).

Letter Shape Sharpeners

Can You See . . .?

Two letter shapes below that are the same?

a f e m n j s y p h d r j

Two letter *pairs* that are the same?

k oo j ee s t ee r oo w

Three letter shapes that look like someone holding both arms up?

b oo j y u y e oo o y h d

Four letters that look like wiggly waves?

w h y w m l r e w x y w

Five letter shapes that are the same?

n y s y n o y d e y u h y

Letter-Talking Tales

Six Letter-Talking Stories follow.

**Each one is accompanied by a picture and a set of games to play.
These activities will teach your child to:**

- **recognize 6 letter shapes and**
- **remember the *sounds* they 'say'.**

Tip 1: How to Read /w/

Remember when you are reading the text, the letters that appear within slashes like this /j/ indicate a ***sound***, the sound associated with that letter. You should pronounce /w/ like the initial sound heard in the word wave, /ee/ like the initial sound heard in the word eel, and so on.

Tip 2: Avoid the /uh/sound

When saying the sounds, avoid the schwa (/uh/) sound: say /j/ as heard at the start of the word jump, not juh.

Tip 3: Letter-sounds that continue

Some letter sounds are known as *continuants* because the sound continues. The sound /z/ says /zzzz/ in one long continuous stream, not /zuh/. The sounds /ee/ and /oo/ are also sounds that continue.

Tip 4: Letter names

You may need to remind your child that when letters 'talk', they do not say their *name*; they make different sounds: /j/, not *jay*, /w/ not *double you*.

Tip 5: Meaning of a tick

If you see a tick in the instructions, it means it's time to praise your child with enthusiasm. Simple, brief encouragements work well. You can just comment, 'Good!' 'Excellent!' 'Yes!' 'Clever!' 'Well done!' 'You're right!' A tick symbol like this: (✓ x 5) indicates the number of times you can praise your child.

Tip 6: Have fun!

There is no pressure to complete the games in a set time. Your pace of game-playing will depend on your child's age and attention span. The main aim is to have fun. Praise or reward often. If your child seems distracted, stop. Play again later on.

Jumping Jack

Praise enthusiastically each time you see a tick symbol (✓)

A Funny Story

Point to the picture opposite and say, 'Here is a funny picture of a new letter shape.' Explain, 'This letter looks like Jack, the jolly jumping joker who jumps out of a Jack-in-the-box toy. Can you trace his shape from the top of his neck down to his shoes?' (✓)

Chat and Cheer

Explain and ask, 'A Jack-in-the box toy has a lid. You turn the handle to play music. Can you find the handle?' (✓) Continue, 'When the music stops – the lid pops open! And out jumps Jack! Can you point to the box?' (✓) Ask, 'Can you point to the lid?' (✓) Ask, 'What happens when the lid pops open?' (Jack jumps out, and he jumps up and down)(✓)

A Sound Mystery

Say, 'I wonder what sound this letter shape makes? Let's read the story to find out' Read the story slowly pronouncing the sound/j/ like the sound you hear at the start of the word *jump*. Read the story again, and pause to point out: the three 'j' shapes, and Jack's jolly smiling face. Ask, '*Why* does this letter shape make a /j/ sound?' (Because it makes a judder-y jumping sound ✓)

Letter Sound

Point to the three letter 'j's in the picture. Ask, 'Do you remember what sound Jack makes when he starts jumping?' Ask, 'Can you make that sound three times? And again?' (✓)

Letter Talk

Ask, 'Can you find all the jumping jack letter shapes in the picture and make their sound each time?' (✓ ✓ ✓ ✓) Ask, 'Can you point and count to all the letters that look like that in the story text?' (x eight ✓)

Letter Hunt

Ask, 'Can you point to the letters below that look like jumping Jack?' (✓ x 4)

o l j i p y j k o l j i j e m

Jumping Jack

/j/ /j/ /j/

Looks like a
Jolly jumping Jack
He loves to . . . .

. . . jump! And jump!
And he's hard to put back!

Happy Me

Funny Picture

Point to the picture opposite and say, 'This funny picture tells the story about *two* letters. When these two letters are side by side together they make just *one* sound.' Ask, 'Can you point to each of the two letters?' (✓✓) Ask, 'Can you find and point to the dimples at the corners of the mouth?' (✓✓)

Chat and Cheer

Say, 'It looks like these two letters are inside someone's mouth. They look a bit like something you would find inside your mouth. What is it?' (teeth)

A Sound Mystery

Ask, 'I wonder what sound these two letters make? Let's read the story to find out.' Read the story slowly. Pronounce the sound /ee/ like the sound you hear in the middle of the word *teeth.* Read the story again and pause to point out the 'two letters' and their 'sounds of glee' coming out of the laughing mouth. Ask, '*Why* do the two letters make the sound /ee/?' (They are laughing ✓)

Letter Sound

Ask, 'Can you point to the laughing sounds coming from the mouth?'(✓✓) 'Can you make these sounds in a laughing voice?' (✓✓)

Letter-Talk

Ask, 'What are *sounds of gle*e? Are they sad crying sounds or happy laughing sounds?' (happy, laughing sounds ✓) Point to all three pairs of /ee/ sounds in the picture, and ask, 'What sound do these two letters make when they are together?' (/ee/ ✓) 'And these two?' (/ee/ ✓) 'And what about these two letters? What sound do they make?' (/ee/ ✓) Ask, 'How many letters in the story can you find that make this sound?' (six ✓)

Letter Hunt

Ask, 'Can you find all the letters below that make that happy laughing sound and make them say their happy sound each time?' (✓✓✓✓)

g m ee c d ee x ee j ee

Happy Me

Look! Can you see?
Two letters by the *name* of 'e'
Together is where they want to be
Can you hear their sound of glee?
Hee - /ee/, /ee/ - /ee/!

Wavy Waves

A Funny Picture

Point to the picture opposite and say, 'Here is a strange picture of another letter shape.' Explain, 'This letter looks a bit like a wiggly wave.' Ask, 'Can you trace the shape from the top left corner with your finger (demonstrate)' . . . 'down, and then up to the top of a wave and back down and up to the top of the next wave?' (✓) 'And, once more?' (✓)

Chat and Cheer

Ask, 'What does this letter look like again?' (a wiggly wave) Ask, 'Can you point to the little waves on top of the sea?' (✓) Ask, 'How many wiggly, wavy letters do you see in the picture in total?' (five ✓)

A Sound Mystery

Say, 'I wonder what *sound* this wiggly letter makes.' Let's read the story to find out!' Read the story slowly. Pronounce the sound /w/ like the sound you hear at the beginning of the word *wave: /w/ not /wuh/*. Read the story a second time and pause after the words *wiggly wave* to trace over the wiggly waves in the picture underneath the big letter shape. Read the five /w/ sounds at the end of the story in a rhythmic, steady fashion. Ask, '*Why* does this letter say/w/?' (Because it makes the steady sound of waves washing to shore ✓)

Letter-Talk

Ask, 'Can you point to all the wiggly letters in the picture and make them say their sound each time?' (✓✓✓✓✓) Ask, 'Can you point to all the wiggly letters in the story and make them say their wishy-washy sound each time?' (✓ x 13)

Letter Hunt

Ask, 'Among the letters below, can you find all the letters that say: /j/'? (✓ x 2) '/ee/'?' (✓ x 2) '/w/?' (✓ x 6)

w s ee j w m e w ee w w j d w

Wavy Waves

/w/ looks wavy
Like a wiggly wave
It washes ashore
To a windy cave
Hear its wish - y, wash - y,
/w/ - /w/ - /w/ - /w/ - /w/!

Spooky /oo/

A Funny Picture

Point to the picture opposite and say, 'Here is a funny picture of a ghost that tells a story about ***two*** letters.' Ask, 'Can you point to the two letters and trace over them?' (the two eyes of the ghost ✓) Explain, 'When these two letters get together and are side by side, they make a new spooky sound.'

Chat and Cheer

Ask, 'Can you point to the ghost's eyes?' (✓) Ask, 'What is strange about the ghost's mouth?' (it is made of *two* round letters) Ask, 'How many times in the picture do you see two round letters side by side?' (three ✓)

A Sound Mystery

Ask, 'I wonder what *sound* the two letters make? Shall we read the story to find out?' Read the story slowly and pronounce the sound /oo/ like the /oo/ sound you hear in the word *boo*. Read the story a second time, and make sure to read the /oo/ sounds in the first and last lines in a spooky (high-pitched, wavering) voice. Point to the sound coming from the ghost's mouth as you read them. Ask. 'Why do these two letters make the sound/oo/?' (Because they sound like a ghost that wants to scare you!)

Letter Sound

Point to the sound the ghost is making and ask, 'Can you make this ghostly sound?' (✓) Ask, 'Can you make that sound again in a high ghostly, wavering voice?' (✓)

Letter-Talk

Ask your child to look at the words in the story and find all the places where the two letters 'oo' say /oo/. Ask, 'How many times did you find that /oo/ sound?' (eight ✓)

Letter Hunt

Ask, 'Among the letters below, can you find all the letters that say /oo/?' (✓ x 3) 'And /ee/?' (✓ x 3)

oo j ee w oo ee z ee oo j w w

Spooky 'oo'

'/oo/ - /oo/ - /oo/'
This spooky ghost
Wants to scare you
So he says,
'/oo/ - oo/ - /oo/ – boo!'

Zig - Zaggy

A Funny Picture

Point to the picture opposite and say, 'Here is another letter shape. It looks just like a zig-zagged line.' Say, 'See if you can trace its shape, starting here' (Point to the left of the top of the shape: trace across, then down on a slant to the lower line and then from left to right.) Help your child trace the shape several times. (✓✓✓)

Chat and Cheer

Explain, 'This letter shape is made up of just three straight lines. Can you point to each of them in turn?' (✓✓✓) Ask, 'Now can you trace the letter shape all by yourself from the top?' (✓) Ask, 'How many letters with this shape do you see in the picture?' (four ✓)

A Sound Mystery

Ask, 'I wonder what sound this letter says? Let's read the story to find out!' Read the story slowly, pronouncing the sound /z/ like the sound you hear at the start of the word *zigzag*. Draw out the sound to say /zzzzzzz/. (Make sure to say /zzz/, not 'zee' or 'zed'.) Pause after the words: *zips, zaps,* and *zooms* to trace over each of the three lines in turn that make up the letter shape. Ask, '*Why* does this letter say /z/?' (It sounds zippy, like a zipper being zipped all the way up ✓)

Letter Sound

Ask, 'Can you make that zig-zaggy sound?' (✓) Ask, 'Can you make the sound last a long time?' (/zzzzzzzzzz/ ✓)

Letter Talk

Ask, 'Can you count how many zigzag-shaped letters are in the picture?' (four ✓) Ask, 'Can you count how many zigzagged letters are in the story?' (eleven ✓) Say, 'Look at the story text again and point and say the zippy /z/ sound each time you find a zig-zaggy letter like that.' (✓ x 11)

Letter Hunt

Ask, 'Among the letters below can you find all the letters that say, /j/? /ee/? /oo/ and /z/?'

j ee w oo z y f z n oo z a b

Zig-Zaggy

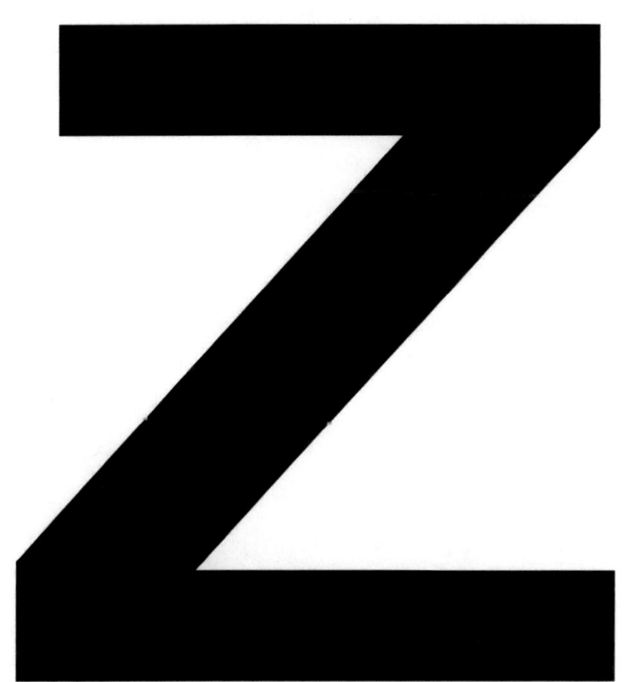

z z z

Here is / z z z/

A zig- zaggy line

Can you hear his

/ z z z / ?

As he zips, zaps and

Zooms along fine?

Yip -Yip Yippee

A Funny Picture

Point to the picture opposite and say, 'This funny picture tells a story about a new letter shape. This letter looks like it has its arms up in the air.' Ask, 'Can you point to its arms?' (✓) Ask, 'Can you trace its shape with your finger?' Demonstrate how to trace over one arm and then the other, and finally, its long tail. Have your child trace its shape several times.

Chat and Cheer

Say, 'Look at the letter opposite again. It looks like the letter is excited and shouting something. Do you think maybe he wants to celebrate? Why do you think that?' (His arms are up in the air) Ask, 'How many letters do see in the picture in total that look like someone celebrating with their arms up?' (five ✓)

A Sound Mystery

Say, 'I wonder what sound this letter makes. Let's read the story to find out!' Read the story slowly. Pronounce the sound /y/ like the sound you hear at the beginning of the word *yippee*. Read the story a second time and then ask, 'What word does the letter say in this story?' (Yippee ✓) Ask, '*Why* do you think this letter sounds like /y/?' (Because the letter shape looks like someone holding both arms up to celebrate and shout *yippee!* ✓)

Letter Sound

Ask, 'What sound does this letter say?' (/y/ ✓) Ask, 'Can you make this sound in a big loud voice three times like you are celebrating something?' (/y/ /y/ /y/! ✓)

Letter-Talk

Ask, 'Can you find all the letters that say /y/ in the story and say their sound each time?' (✓ x 7)

Letter Hunt

Ask, 'Among the letters below, can you find all the letters that say, /y/?' (✓ x 5) '/z/?' (✓ x 5) '/j/?' (✓ x 2)

y s z t z w z z y j z y y j w y

Yip -Yip Yipee

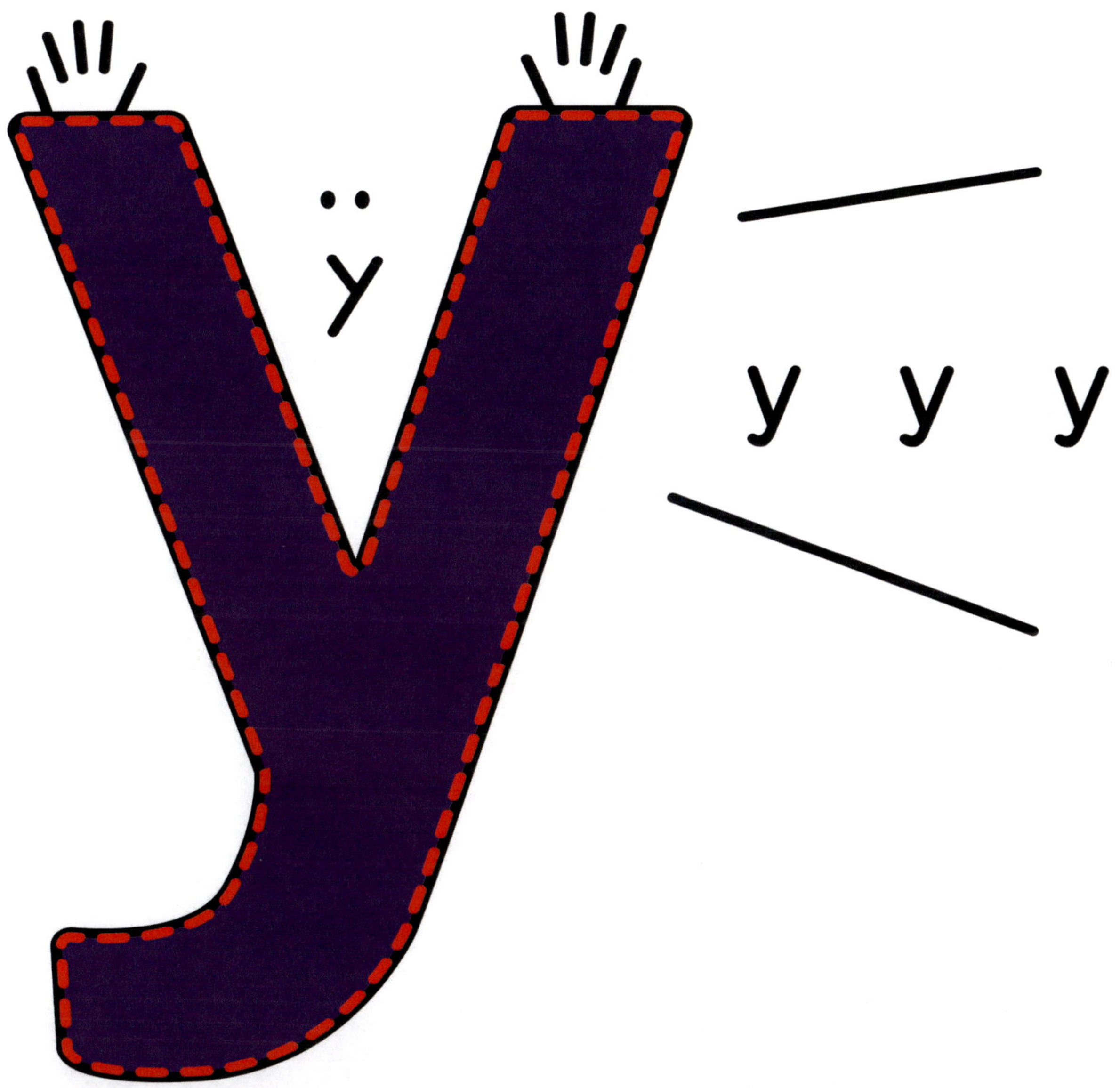

/y/ as you can see
Has both arms up
And he yips,
'/y/ - /y/ - /y/ -
Yippee !'

Seek and Speak

PART ONE: REVIEW THE LETTER-TALKING PICTURES (PP 12-23).

1) Looks Like: Ask, 'Can you find a picture where the letter or letters *look like*: a zig-zag line/ Jack jumping out of a box/ a wiggly wave/ a pair of eyes/ a pair of teeth in a laughing mouth/ a person holding both arms up yelling *Yippee*?'

2) It Says: Point to various letters on these pages and ask, 'What does this letter *say*?'

3) Why: Point to various letters and ask *why* questions: '*Why* does this letter say /j/ /ee/ /w/ /oo/ /z/ /y/?'

PART TWO: POINT TO THE SIX SMALLER PICTURES ABOVE.

Ask the three kinds of *Seek and Speak* questions once more.

Giant Seek and Speak

Point to the various letters at random and ask, 'Do you remember what this letter ***says***?' Continue until your child can remember what sound each of the letters say without hesitation.

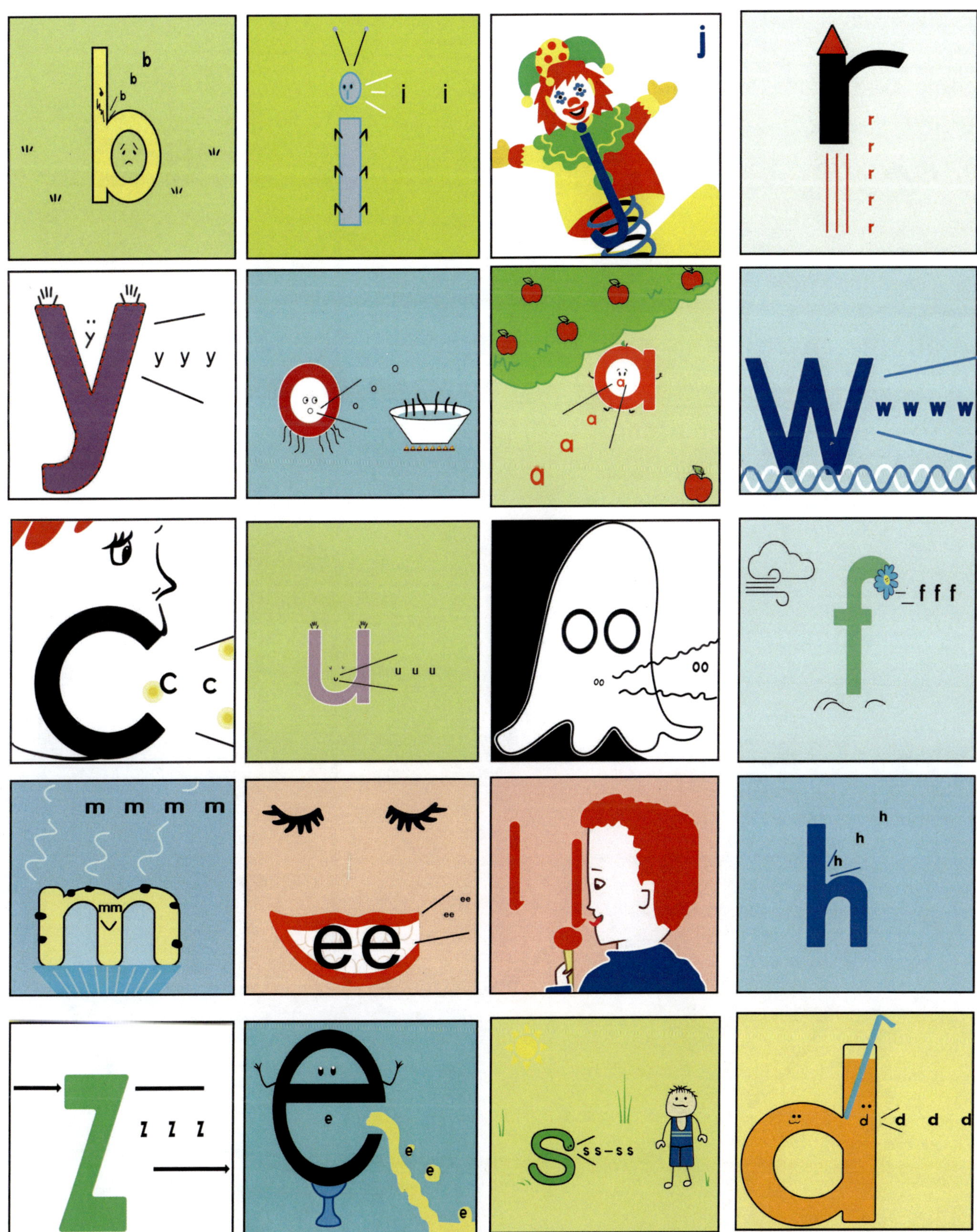

Lightning Letter-Sounds

INSIDE 'J' Take turns to say the sounds from the top line.

OOH HOW MANY? Count how many /OO/sounds. (six ✓)

SEE ME? How many /ee/ sounds can you see. (six ✓)

DOT ON TOP Can you read the name in the dot on top?

TOP TO TAIL Try to say all the sounds from the top.

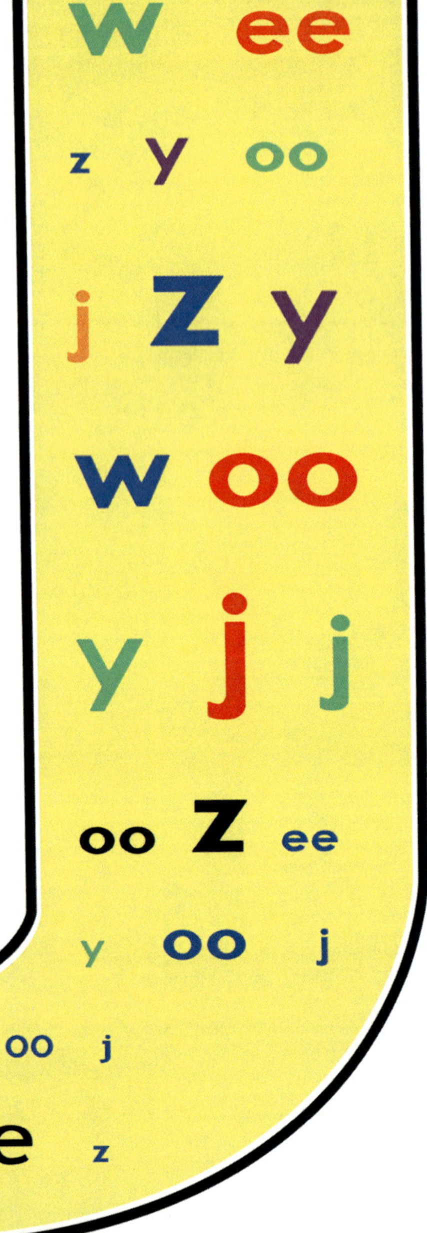

Mind Bending Blending

One, Two, Three Magic!

Take the 3 sounding out steps to make magic: 1) say one sound, 2) say two sounds together, 3) repeat the two sounds together or more, wave a magic wand (wooden spoon, ruler) and add the last sound to say the word! Magic!

1	2	3	★
j	je	je t	jet
j	jo	jo g	jog
j	ja	ja m	jam
j	ju	ju g	jug
j	ju	jum p	jump

Once your child can read each word well, ask, 'Can you find its matching picture?'

Wiggly Eel

- Take the sounding out steps to say the word.
- Find the matching picture.

1	2			3
ee	ee + l			eel
s	s + ee			see
b	b + ee			bee
w	wi	wi	+ g	wig
w	we	we	+ t	wet
f	foo	foo	+ l	fool

Wickedly Wily Word Reading

Green Grass

- Ask your child to choose a number between 1 and 6 and find the number below.
- To begin with, make the sound of the initial consonant blend for your child to copy: /sn/, /tr/, /gr/, /tw/, /sl/, /cl/.
- Then help your child read all the words in the line.
- When fluent, ask, 'Which word best matches the picture?' (✓ Reward)

1) **snip snack snooze* sneeze***

2) **truck tree trick trip**

3) **grab green grip grass**

4) **tweets twits twins twigs**

5) **slam slip sleep slug**

6) **cliff club clap clam**

(* Tell your child the /e/ at the end of the word is silent.)

Zigzag Zoo

(**This *spelling* game will super-charge your child's reading!**)

- First ask, 'What animals do you see in the zoo below?' (help your child to name them)
- Ask, 'Can you find two pictures which show *two* animals?' (✓✓yaks and roos)
- Ask, 'Can you choose a zoo animal below and tell me what it is?' (✓) Now ask your child to say the sounds in the name very slowly as you point to the spaces above the picture.
- Point to the list of animals printed below left, and ask. 'Were you right?'

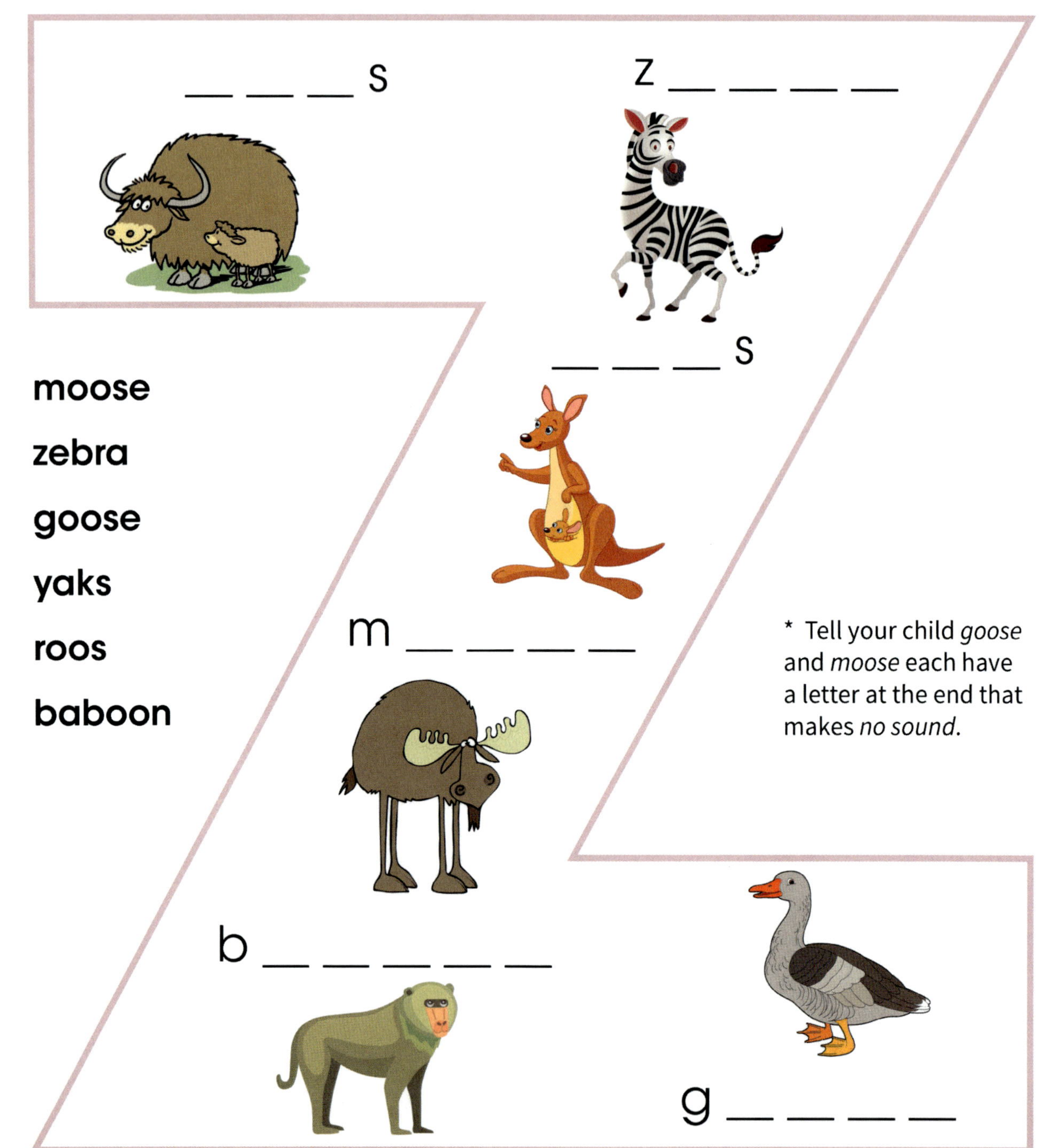

* Tell your child *goose* and *moose* each have a letter at the end that makes *no sound.*

Peek-A-Boo:
The Book Cover (next page)

- Help your child sound out and read the title of the book.
- Discuss the three pictures on the book cover.
- Help your child read the words under the pictures.

Inside the Book - Games to Play

COVER UP all the pictures and play these games:

1) **Twice:** Help your child sound out and read the four words (phrases/ sentences) on a page at least twice.

2) **Turns:** Take turns pointing to one of the words (phrases/ sentences) for the other player to read.

UNCOVER all the pictures and play this game:

3) **Matching:** Ask your child to read the four choices (words/ phrases/ sentences) and find their matching pictures.

About Tricky Words

- As in *Cal a Cat* (Step 3 reading book), Tricky Words are <u>underlined</u>.
- If your child reads an underlined word ask, 'Does that word sound a bit strange?'
- Remind your child that this is a 'Tricky' word. Say, 'It doesn't follow the sounding out rules very well. It wants to try and trick you!'
- Say, 'To get some help with it, look to see if this word is on the last page.' (Show your child page 9).
- Then say, 'Oh yes! There *are* some tricky words. How many?' (five ✓)
- Point to the words below and say, 'This version of the words tells you what they say if they *had* followed the rules and were easy to sound out. For example, in the word *trees* (point to it) the /s/ at the end sounds like a /z/' (point to the version underneath the word *trees*).
- Point to the word ***I*** and say, 'This word is a big capital letter for the sound /i/. But because it's a capital letter, it feels VERY important. Instead of saying its sound, /i/, it says its *name* , I.'

Peek-A-Boo

peek

wet

zoo

Say the sounds **j ee w oo z y**

jam

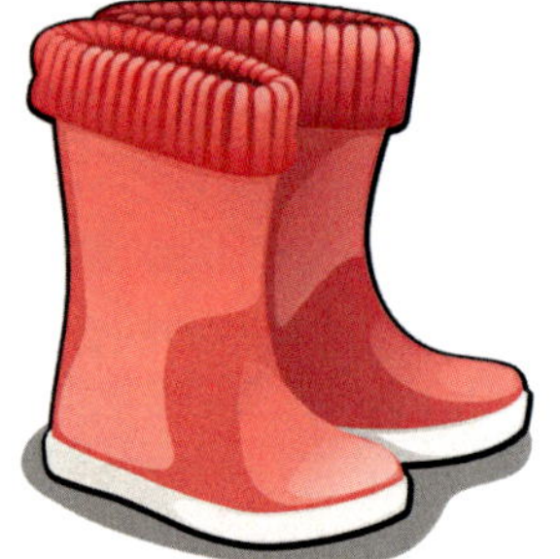

wok

peek

boots

I

win

wind

wed

wag

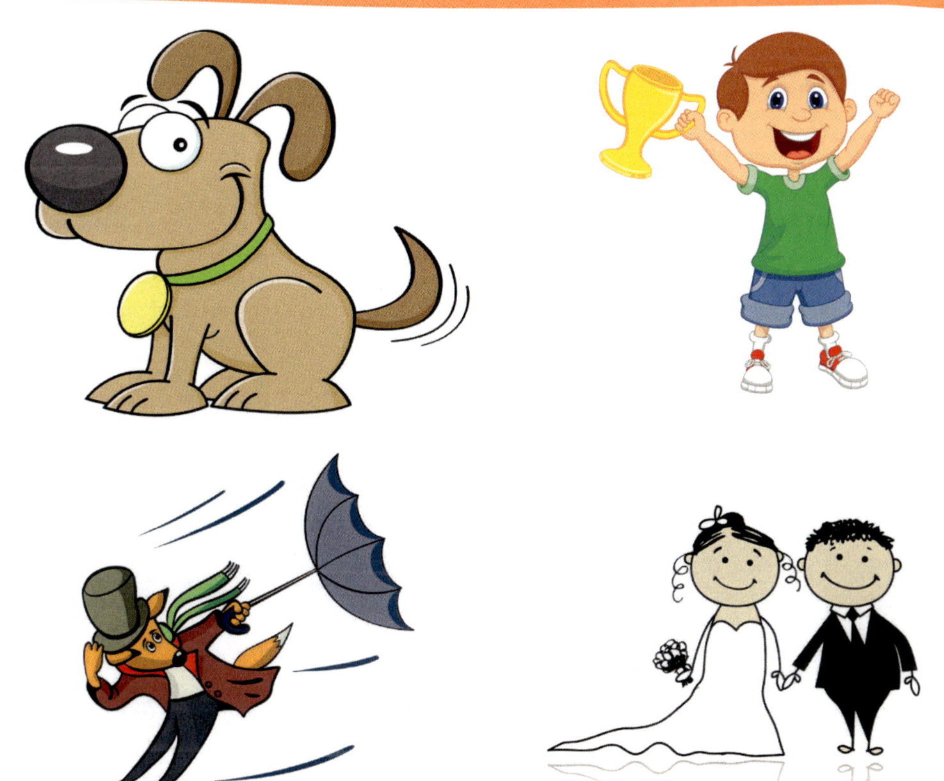

2

hoops

zigzags

spoons

<u>trees</u>

3

Jill weeps.

Zac winks.

Ben yells.

A cat sleeps.

4

wet web

a green jeep

a steep hill

pink fizz

5

A jet zooms.

Liz swims.

A dog jumps.

Will speeds.

6

a tree on a cliff

kids on a roof

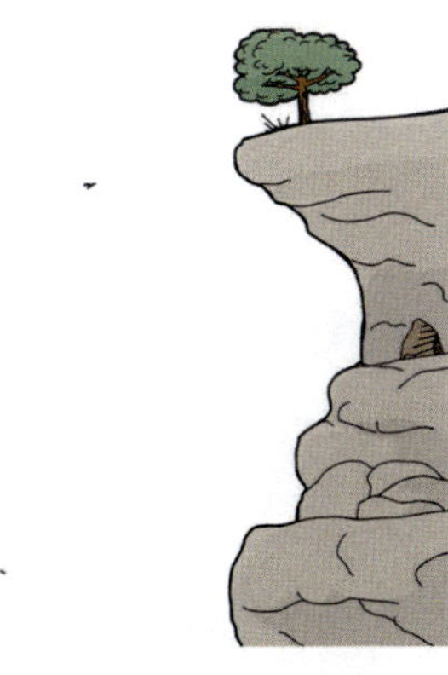

a frog in reeds

twins in green

7

I see feet.

I see a moose.

I see a baboon.

I see a raccoon.

8

Tricky Words in this Book

trees	speeds	reeds	I	moose
/treez/	/speedz/	/reedz/	I	/moos/

9

A Book to Read:

2) 1,2,3 Swim in the Pool

- Help your child read the title of the book. Tell your child the new tricky word *the*.
- Discuss what your child can see in the picture.
- Point to the lower half of the page. Explain, 'There are three sentences here. Each one starts with a capital letter and ends with a period.'
- Ask your child, 'Can you find a capital letter at the start of each sentence and a period at the end?' (✓✓✓)
- Help your child read each of the sentences until he is able to read them without help. Praise enthusiastically.

THE 1, 2, 3 GAME:

- When your child can read each page well, say, 'It's time to play the 1, 2, 3 Game!'
- Point to the numbers and ask, 'Can you point to sentence number 1?' Continue until your child can point to all the sentences by their number.
- Point to the picture below the sentences. Ask, 'When you read the sentences, can you figure out which sentence (number 1, 2, or 3) best matches this picture?'
- When your child has selected a number, turn to page J, the Answer Key, where the answers for pages A to I are listed. Show your child how to check his answer. Next to the A page, there is a sentence number. Is this the number your child selected?
- Play this game for all the other pages.

TRICKY WORDS

When your child encounters underlined, Tricky Words, let him check the back cover of the booklet. This shows how the words should be spelled if they followed normal sounding out rules.

SHOW OFF

Let your child read the story and check his answers on his own.

I, 2, 3 Swim in the Pool

1 The cat sits in the sun.
2 Liz sips a drink.
3 Jack, the dog, sleeps.

1, 2, 3?

A

1 Liz <u>is</u> too hot.
2 Liz slips <u>into</u> the cool pool.
3 Jack, the dog, can see Liz.

1, 2, 3?

B

1 Buzz, the cat, still sleeps.
2 But Jack jumps up.
3 Jack is too hot.

1, 2, 3?

C

1 Jack yips and yelps.
2 He jumps in the pool to see Liz.
3 Soon Liz feels too cool.

1, 2, 3?

D

1 Liz sits in the hot sun.
2 Buzz sleeps in the grass.
3 Jack swims and swims.

1, 2, 3?

E

1 Soon Jack stands in the sun.
2 He feels too wet.
3 Eek! See Jack's trick!

1, 2, 3?

F

1 Buzz, the cat, got wet.
2 He is in a bad mood.
3 Liz got wet too.

1, 2, 3?

G

1 Liz feeds Buzz.
2 Soon Buzz feels snug.
3 Jack <u>has</u> <u>his</u> food too.

1, 2, 3?

H

1 Jack feels well.
2 Soon . . . he is asleep.
3 And Liz has a snooze too.

1, 2, 3?

I

Answer Key

A - 2, B - 2, C -1, D - 2, E - 3, F - 3, G -2, H - 3, I - 2

Tricky Words in this Book

The	the	is	into	He	to	has	his
(thu)	(thu)	(iz)	(in-too)	(hee)	(too)	(haz)	(hiz)

Meena Moose

Colour Me!

CONGRATULATIONS!

____

(name of child)

is a **STEP 4** Super Reader!

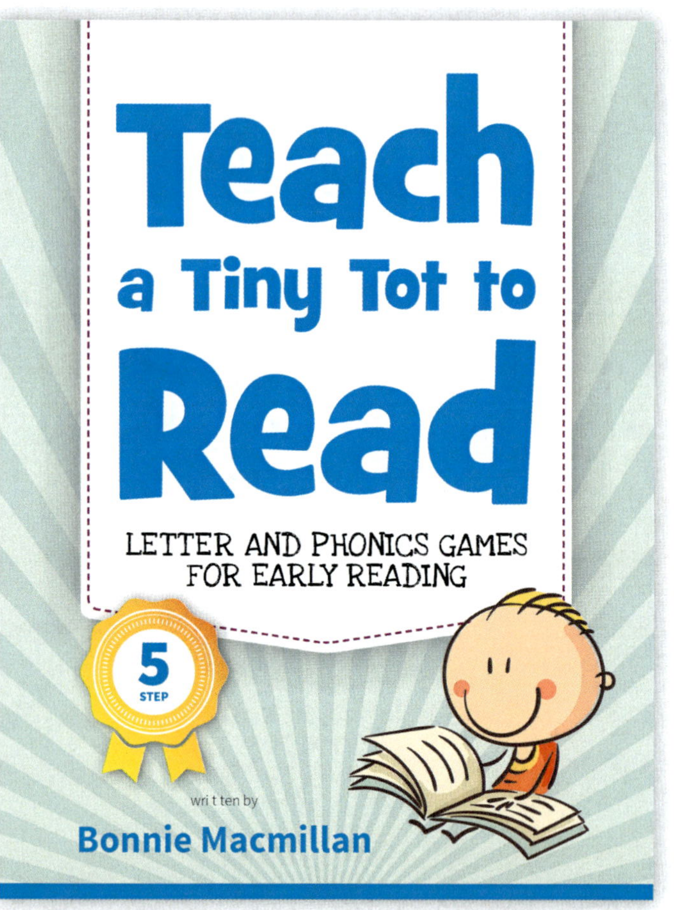

Made in the USA
Middletown, DE
15 September 2023